PAT
PAT
PAT
PAT

zzzzz

PAT
PAT
PAT
PAT

Published in 2015 by Hardie Grant Books, an imprint of Hardie Grant Publishing

Hardie Grant Books (Melbourne)
Building 1, 658 Church Street
Richmond, Victoria 3121
hardiegrantbooks.com.au

Hardie Grant Books (London)
5th & 6th Floors
52–54 Southwark Street
London SE1 1RU
hardiegrantbooks.co.uk

A Cataloguing-in-Publication entry is available from the catalogue of the National Library of Australia at www.nla.gov.au

The Wisdom of Prince Philip
ISBN 9781743790755

Publishing Director: Paul McNally
Design Manager: Mark Campbell
Illustrator: Oslo Davis
Production Manager: Todd Rechner

Printed in Spain by Estellaprint

The
Wisdom
of
Prince Philip

Antony A. Butt
with illustrations by Oslo Davis

hardie grant books

"You managed not to get eaten then?"

To a British student who had trekked in Papua New Guinea, during an official visit in 1998.

"Ghastly."

Prince Philip's opinion of Beijing, during a 1986 tour of China.

"Ghastly."

Prince Philip's opinion of Stoke-on-Trent, as
offered to the city's Labour MP Joan Walley
at Buckingham Palace in 1997.

"If it has four legs and it is not a chair, if it has got two wings and it flies but is not an aeroplane and if it swims and it is not a submarine, the Cantonese will eat it."

Said to a World Wildlife Fund meeting in 1986.

"How do you keep the natives off the booze long enough to pass the test?"

Asked of a Scottish driving instructor in 1995.

"You can't have been here that long –
you haven't got a pot belly."

To a British tourist during a tour of Budapest
in Hungary, 1993.

"You ARE a woman, aren't you?"

To a woman in Kenya in 1984, after accepting a gift.

*"We don't come here for our health.
We can think of other ways of
enjoying ourselves."*

During a trip to Canada in 1976.

*"Deaf? If you're near there,
no wonder you are deaf."*

Said to a group of deaf children standing near
a Caribbean steel drum band in 2000.

"What do you gargle with – pebbles?"

To Tom Jones, after the Royal Variety Performance,
1969. He added the following day: "It is very
difficult at all to see how it is possible to become
immensely valuable by singing what I think are
the most hideous songs."

"A few years ago, everybody was saying we must have more leisure, everyone's working too much. Now that everybody's got more leisure time they are complaining they are unemployed. People don't seem to make up their minds what they want."

A man of the people shares insight into the recession that gripped Britain in 1981.

"British women can't cook."

Winning the hearts of the Scottish Women's
Institute in 1961.

"People usually say that after a fire it is water damage that is the worst. We are still drying out Windsor Castle."

To survivors of the Lockerbie bombings in 1993.

"It was part of the fortunes of war. We didn't have counsellors rushing around every time somebody let off a gun, asking, 'Are you all right – are you sure you don't have a ghastly problem?' You just got on with it!"

On the issue of stress counselling for servicemen in a TV documentary marking the 50th Anniversary of V-J Day in 1995.

*"It looks as though it was put
in by an Indian."*

The Prince's verdict of a fuse box during a tour of a
Scottish factory in August 1999. He later clarified
his comment: "I meant to say cowboys. I just got
my cowboys and Indians mixed up."

"If you stay here much longer, you will go home with slitty eyes."

To 21-year-old British student Simon Kerby during a visit to China in 1986.

*"Do you know they have eating dogs
for the anorexic now?"*

To a wheelchair-bound Susan Edwards, and her
guide dog Natalie in 2002.

"Don't feed your rabbits pawpaw fruit – it acts as a contraceptive. Then again, it might not work on rabbits."

Giving advice to a Caribbean rabbit breeder
in Anguilla in 1994.

"Aren't most of you descended from pirates?"

In the Cayman Islands, 1994.

"I have never been noticeably reticent about talking on subjects about which I know nothing."

Addressing a group of industrialists in 1961.

*"If you travel as much as we do
you appreciate the improvements in
aircraft design of less noise and more
comfort – provided you don't travel
in something called economy class,
which sounds ghastly."*

To the Aircraft Research Association in 2002.

"And what exotic part of the world do you come from?"

Asked in 1999 of Tory politician Lord Taylor of Warwick, whose parents are Jamaican. He replied: "Birmingham."

"Young people are the same as they always were. They are just as ignorant."

At the 50th anniversary of the Duke of Edinburgh Awards scheme.

"Oh no, I might catch some ghastly disease."

On a visit to Australia in 1992, when asked if he wanted to stroke a koala bear.

*"Ah you're the one who wrote the letter.
So you can write then? Ha, ha!
Well done."*

Meeting 14-year-old George Barlow, who invited
the Queen to visit Romford, Essex, in 2003.

"Were you here in the bad old days? ...
That's why you can't read and
write then!"

To parents during a visit to Fir Vale Comprehensive
School in Sheffield, which had from a suffered
poor academic reputation.

"I wish he'd turn the microphone off!"

The Prince expresses his opinion of Elton John's
performance at the 73rd Royal Variety Show, 2001.

"If a cricketer, for instance, suddenly decided to go into a school and batter a lot of people to death with a cricket bat, which he could do very easily, I mean, are you going to ban cricket bats?"

In a Radio 4 interview shortly after the Dunblane shootings in 1996. He said to the interviewer off-air afterwards: "That will really set the cat among the pigeons, won't it?"

"I would like to go to Russia very much – although the bastards murdered half my family."

In 1967, asked if he would like to visit the Soviet Union.

"It's a vast waste of space."

Philip entertained guests in 2000 at the reception
of a new £18m British Embassy in Berlin, which
the Queen had just opened.

*"There's a lot of your family
in tonight."*

After glancing at business chief Atul Patel's
name badge during a 2009 Buckingham Palace
reception for 400 influential British Indians
to meet the Royal couple.

"The problem with London is the tourists. They cause the congestion. If we could just stop the tourism, we could stop the congestion."

At the opening of City Hall in 2002.

"You could do with losing a little bit of weight."

To hopeful astronaut, 13-year-old Andrew Adams.

"Any bloody fool can lay a wreath at the thingamy."

Discussing his role in an interview with
Jeremy Paxman.

"During the Blitz a lot of shops had their windows blown in and sometimes they put up notices saying, 'More open than usual.' I now declare this place more open than usual."

Unveiling a plaque at the University
of Hertfordshire's new Hatfield campus
in November 2003.

"Ah, so this is feminist corner then."

Joining a group of female Labour MPs, who
were wearing name badges reading "Ms", at
a Buckingham Palace drinks party in 2000.

"A pissometer?"

The Prince sees, then renames, the piezometer
water gauge demonstrated by Australian farmer
Steve Filelti in 2000.

"Get me a beer. I don't care what kind it is, just get me a beer!"

On being offered the finest Italian wines by PM Giuliano Amato at a dinner in Rome in 2000.

Later that night...

"Your country is one of the most notorious centres of trading in endangered species."

Accepting a conservation award in Thailand in 1991.

"You must be out of your minds."

To Solomon Islanders, on being told that their population growth was 5 per cent a year, in 1982.

*"Do you still throw spears
at each other?"*

♛

Prince Philip shocks Aboriginal leader William
Brin at the Aboriginal Cultural Park
in Queensland, 2002.

"Oh! You are the people ruining the rivers and the environment."

To three young employees of a Scottish fish farm at Holyrood Palace in 1999.

"Oh, it's you that owns that ghastly car is it? We often see it when driving to Windsor Castle."

To neighbour Elton John after hearing he had sold his Watford FC–themed Aston Martin in 2001.

"No, I would probably end up spitting it out over everybody."

Prince Philip declines the offer of some fish from Rick Stein's seafood deli in 2000.

"The French don't know how to cook breakfast."

After a breakfast of bacon, eggs, smoked salmon, kedgeree, croissants and pain au chocolat – from Gallic chef Regis Crépy – in 2002.

"Where's the Southern Comfort?"

On being presented with a hamper of southern
goods by the American ambassador in London
in 1999.

"Do people trip over you?"

Meeting a wheelchair-bound nursing-home resident
in 2002.

"The man who invented the red carpet needed his head examined."

To hosts (on a red carpet) during a state visit to Brazil in 1968.

"You have mosquitoes.
I have the press."

To the matron of a hospital in the Caribbean
in 1966.

"Dontopedalogy is the science of opening your mouth and putting your foot in it, a science which I have practised for a good many years."

Address to the General Dental Council, quoted in *Time* in 1960.

"I don't think a prostitute is more moral than a wife, but they are doing the same thing."

Dismissing claims that those who sell slaughtered meat have greater moral authority than those who participate in blood sports, in 1988.

"That's a nice tie ... Do you have any knickers in that material?"

Discussing the tartan designed for the Papal visit with then–Scottish Tory leader Annabel Goldie in 2010.

"In education, if in nothing else, the Scotsman knows what is best for him. Indeed, only a Scotsman can really survive a Scottish education."

Said when he was made Chancellor of the University of Edinburgh in November 1953.

*"Why don't you go and live in a hostel
to save cash?"*

Asked of a penniless student.

"So who's on drugs here?... HE looks as if he's on drugs."

To a 14-year-old member of a Bangladeshi youth club in 2002.

"I don't know how they are going to integrate in places like Glasgow and Sheffield."

After meeting students from Brunei coming to Britain to study in 1998.

"Holidays are curious things, aren't they? You send children to school to get them out of your hair. Then they come back and make life difficult for parents. That is why holidays are set so they are just about the limit of your endurance."

At the opening of a school in 2000.

"It's not a very big one, but at least it's dead and it took an awful lot of killing!"

Speaking about a crocodile he shot in Gambia in 1957.

"I must be the only person in Britain glad to see the back of that plane."

Philip did not approve of the noise Concorde made while flying over Buckingham Palace.

"People think there's a rigid class system here, but dukes have even been known to marry chorus girls. Some have even married Americans."

In 2000.

"You're not wearing mink knickers, are you?"

Philip charms fashion writer Serena French at a World Wildlife Fund gathering in 1993.

"All money nowadays seems to be produced with a natural homing instinct for the Treasury."

Bemoaning the rate of British tax in 1963.

"We go into the red next year ... I shall probably have to give up polo."

Comment on US television in 1969 about the Royal Family's finances.

*"If it doesn't fart or eat hay,
she isn't interested."*

Of his daughter, Princess Anne.

"It doesn't look like much work goes on at this University."

Overheard at the University of Bristol's engineering facility. It had been closed so that he and the Queen could officially open it in 2005.

"They're not mating are they?"

Spotting two robots bumping in to one another
at the Science Museum in 2000.

"It is my invariable custom to say something flattering to begin with so that I shall be excused if by any chance I put my foot in it later on."

Full marks for honesty, from a speech in 1956.

"You're just a silly little Whitehall twit: you don't trust me and I don't trust you."

Said to Sir Rennie Maudslay, Keeper of the Privy Purse, in the 1970s.

*"This could only happen in
a technical college."*

On getting stuck in a lift between two floors at
Heriot-Watt University, 1958.

"There was a great improvement in things like trains running on time and building. There was a sense of hope after the depressing chaos of the Weimar Republic."

Explaining the attraction of the Nazis to an American academic in 2006.

"Reichskanzler."

Prince Philip used Hitler's title to address
German chancellor Helmut Kohl during
a speech in Hanover in 1997.

"It looks like the kind of thing my daughter would bring back from her school art lessons."

On being shown "primitive" Ethiopian art in 1965.

"Bugger the table plan, give me my dinner!"

Showing his impatience to be fed at a dinner party in 2004.

*"Can you tell the difference
between them?"*

On being told by President Obama that he'd
had breakfast with the leaders of the UK,
China and Russia.

"I thought it was against the law these days for a woman to solicit."

Said to a woman solicitor.

*"It makes you all look like
Dracula's daughters!"*

To pupils at Queen Anne's School in Reading,
who wear blood-red uniforms, in 1998.

"Well, you didn't design your beard too well, did you? You really must try better with your beard."

To a young fashion designer at Buckingham Palace in 2009.

"It looks like a tart's bedroom."

On seeing plans for the Duke and then–Duchess
of York's house at Sunninghill Park.

"What about Tom Jones? He's made a million and he's a bloody awful singer."

Response to a comment at a small-business lunch about how difficult it is in Britain to get rich.

"Cats kill far more birds than men. Why don't you have a slogan: 'Kill a cat and save a bird?'"

On being told of a project to protect turtle doves in Anguilla in 1965.

"Well, that's more than you know about anything else then."

Speaking, a touch condescendingly, to Michael Buerk, after being told by the BBC newsreader that he did know about the Duke of Edinburgh's Gold Awards in 2004.

"My son ... er ... owns them."

On being asked on a Canadian tour whether
he knew the Scilly Isles.

"The only active sport, which I follow, is polo – and most of the work's done by the pony!"

———

1965

"I'd much rather have stayed in the Navy, frankly."

When asked what he felt about his life in 1992.